MATH COMPUTATION & PROBLEM SOLVING
Grades K-1

Inventive Exercises to Sharpen Skills and Raise Achievement

Series Concept & Development
by Imogene Forte & Marjorie Frank
Exercises by Sharon Gell

Incentive Publications, Inc.
Nashville, Tennessee

About the cover:
Bound resist, or tie dye, is the most ancient known method of fabric surface design. The brilliance of the basic tie dye design on this cover reflects the possibilities that emerge from the mastery of basic skills.

Illustrated by Kathleen Bullock
Cover art by Mary Patricia Deprez, dba Tye Dye Mary®
Cover design by Marta Drayton, Joe Shibley, and W. Paul Nance
Edited by Anna Quinn

ISBN 0-86530-387-8

PRINTED IN THE UNITED STATES OF AMERICA

TABLE OF CONTENTS

Appendix

CELEBRATE BASIC MATH SKILLS

Basic does not mean boring! There is certainly nothing dull about . . .

> . . . deciding how many sardines can fit into a ballpark
>
> . . . counting sports books before the bookworm can eat them
>
> . . . figuring out who will win races between swamp serpents and ladybugs
>
> . . . practicing facts by throwing mud pies or riding a skateboard
>
> . . . solving problems about a wild ride on a bobsled or a river raft
>
> . . . using math facts to help with a rat race, a tug-of-war, or an ice-carving contest
>
> . . . looking for lost golf balls in a swamp or lost boots in a spider web

The idea of celebrating the basics is just what it sounds like—enjoying and improving the skills of computation and problem solving. Each page of this book invites young learners to try a high-interest, visually appealing exercise that will sharpen one math skill. This is not just any ordinary fill-in-the-blanks way to learn. These exercises are fun and surprising, and they make good use of thinking skills. Students will do the useful work of practicing math skills while they enjoy delightful sports and recreation adventures with animals.

This book can be used in many ways:

- to review or practice a math skill with one student
- to sharpen the skill with a small or large group
- to start off a lesson on a particular skill
- to assess how well a student has mastered a skill

Each page has directions that are written simply. It is intended that an adult be available to help students read the information on the page, if help is needed. In most cases, the pages will best be used as a follow-up to a lesson or concept that has been taught. The pages are excellent tools for immediate reinforcement of a concept.

As your students take on the challenges of these adventures with math, they will grow! And as you watch them check off the basic math skills they've acquired or strengthened, you can celebrate with them.

The Skills Test

Use the skills test beginning on page 58 as a pretest and/or a post-test. This will help you check the students' mastery of math skills. You will discover what they have learned or what they will need to practice.

SKILLS CHECKLIST
MATH COMPUTATION & PROBLEM SOLVING, GRADES K-1

✔	SKILL	PAGE(S)
	Add sets of objects	10, 12
	Answer questions from diagrams and pictures	10–13, 23, 39–44, 51
	Subtract sets of objects	11
	Use addition and subtraction facts through 20	13–20
	Add whole numbers	10, 12–16, 19–29, 31–33, 35–38
	Subtract whole numbers	11, 13, 15, 17, 18, 20–27, 34, 35, 38
	Find missing numbers in number sentences	21–26, 53
	Recognize fact families; find missing facts	21, 22
	Write number sentences to match models	23, 24, 39
	Add and subtract with zero	27
	Add 3 numbers	28, 29
	Add and subtract 10	36, 37, 38
	Add 2-digit numbers	31, 32, 33, 35, 36
	Subtract 2-digit numbers	34, 35
	Add and subtract multiples of 10	37, 38
	Choose correct operation for a problem	30
	Identify value of coins	40–42
	Identify amounts of money	39–42
	Solve problems with money	39–42
	Do a variety of time-telling tasks	43–47
	Solve problems with time	43–47
	Use a variety of problem-solving strategies	39–57
	Answer questions from data on graphs and charts	48, 49, 50
	Solve simple word problems	52, 53, 54
	Explain how a problem was solved	56, 57

MATH COMPUTATION
& PROBLEM SOLVING
Grades K-1

Skills Exercises

She Sells Seashells

What a surprise! An octopus is selling seashells on the seashore!
Leo comes out of the water to look at Sandy's shells.

Count the shells in each box.

Then help Leo solve the problems.

Write the missing numbers.

1. 🐚 + ⭐ = ☐   2. 🐚 + 🐚 = ☐

3. 🐚 + 🐚 = ☐   4. ✳ + 🐚 = ☐

Name _____

Add Sets

Jingo's Short Jog

Oh, oh! Jingo forgot about his jogging!
He stopped to look at the animals
along the way.

As he watched, some of them
crawled or flew away.

How many are left?

Jingo saw two lizards. One crawled away.

$-$ ⬡ $=$ $\boxed{1}$

Write the answers.

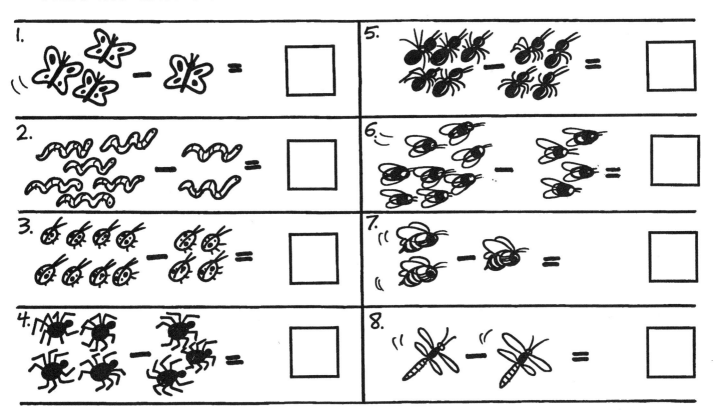

Name _____

Copyright ©1998 by Incentive Publications, Inc., Nashville T^N
Basic Skills/Math K-1

Subtract Sets

Lost Golf Balls

Dizzy and Daisy Dinosaur are looking for golf balls in the swamp.
Help them count the golf balls.
Then answer the questions.

1. How many golf balls are in the water? ☐

2. How many balls are in their hands? ☐

3. How many are on the land? ☐

4. Can you write a number sentence to tell the story?

   ☐ on the land + ☐ in the water + ☐ in hand = ☐ golf balls

Color the animals and the golf balls.

Name _____

Add with Sets

Basic Skills/Math K-1

Ladybug Race

Help the ladybug teams finish their race.
The bug with the most spots will be the winner.
Add or subtract the number of spots on the bugs.
Draw the right number of spots on each answer bug.
Write the total number of spots in the score box.

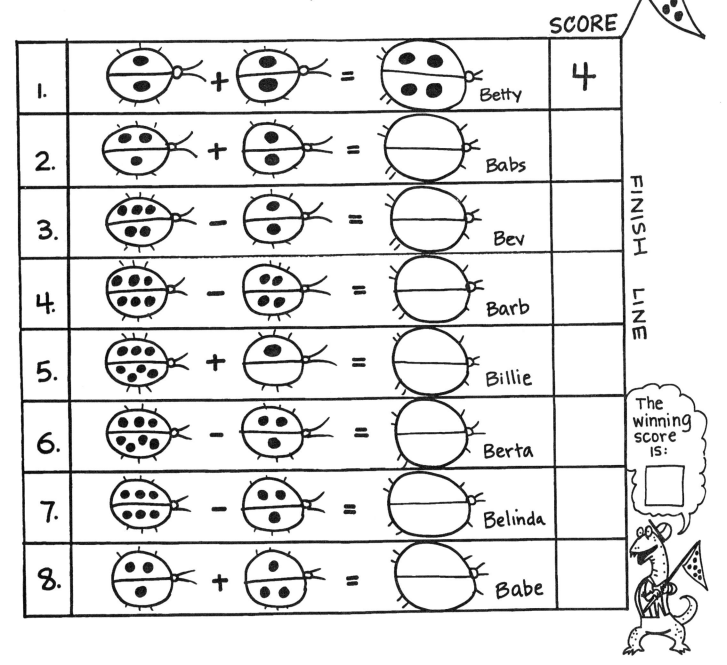

FINISH LINE

The winning score is:

Name _____

Addition & Subtraction Facts through 7

Lost in the Web

Spiro Spider has lots of shoes caught in his web.
Help him find his lost hiking boot.
Write all the answers to the problems.
Then use the **Color Code** to color the shoes and boots.

The red boot is the one Spiro has lost.

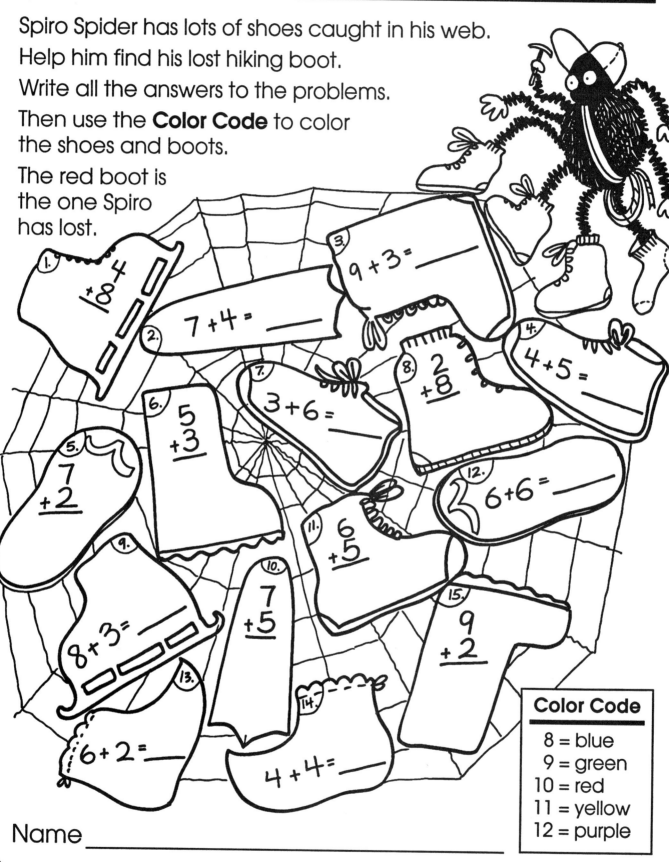

1. 4
   $+8$

2. $7 + 4 =$ _____

3. $9 + 3 =$ _____

4. $4 + 5 =$ _____

5. 7
   $+2$

6. 5
   $+3$

7. $3 + 6 =$ _____

8. 2
   $+8$

9. $8 + 3 =$ _____

10. 7
    $+5$

11. 6
    $+5$

12. $6 + 6 =$ _____

13. $6 + 2 =$ _____

14. $4 + 4 =$ _____

15. 9
    $+2$

Color Code

8 =	blue
9 =	green
10 =	red
11 =	yellow
12 =	purple

Name _____

Addition Facts through 12

Lost Marbles

Suzie's favorite game is marbles.

She has invited 7 friends to join her for a game.

She started the first game with 12 marbles.

She lost 3 marbles.

Now she has 9 marbles, because $12 - 3 = 9$.

Use math facts you know to fill in the missing numbers in the chart.

	Marbles To Start	Marbles Lost	Marbles Left
Suzie had	12	3	9
Elvis had	9	8	
Dino had	11	4	
Dinah had	8	5	
Danny had		7	5
Sally had		6	6
Emma had	11		6
Rico had		3	7

Write the answers.

1. Danny started with ☐ marbles.

2. Emma lost ☐ marbles.

3. Dino finished with ☐ marbles.

4. Sally started with ☐ marbles.

5. Rico started with ☐ marbles.

6. ☐ lost the most marbles.

Name _____

Addition & Subtraction Facts through 12

Fishy Facts

Felix has been fishing for facts. He has a great catch!
Write the answers for all the fishy facts.
Then use the **Color Code** to color Felix's fish.

Color Code

14 = red
15 = green
16 = blue
17 = orange
18 = purple

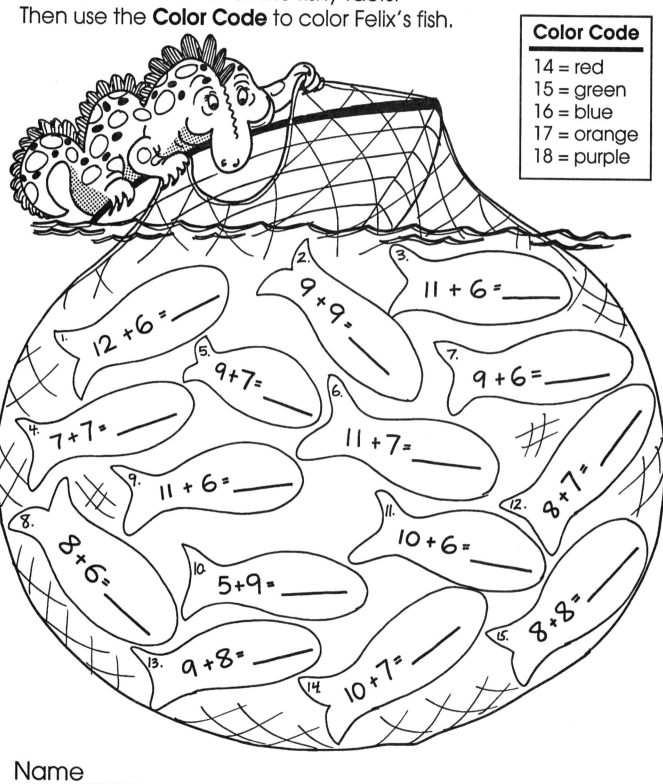

1. 12 + 6 = _____
2. 9 + 9 = _____
3. 11 + 6 = _____
4. 7 + 7 = _____
5. 9 + 7 = _____
6. _____
7. 9 + 6 = _____
8. 8 + 6 = _____
9. 11 + 6 = _____
10. 5 + 9 = _____
11. 10 + 6 = _____
12. 8 + 7 = _____
13. 9 + 8 = _____
14. 10 + 7 = _____
15. 8 + 8 = _____

11 + 7 = _____

Name _____

Addition Facts through 18

Basic Skills/Math K-1

The Mud Pie Fight

It is such fun for Lulu and Larry to throw mud pies!
Finish the facts on the mud pies to find out who threw the most.
Lulu's pies have answers that are even numbers.
Larry's have answers that are odd numbers.
Count the pies and write the scores in the score box.

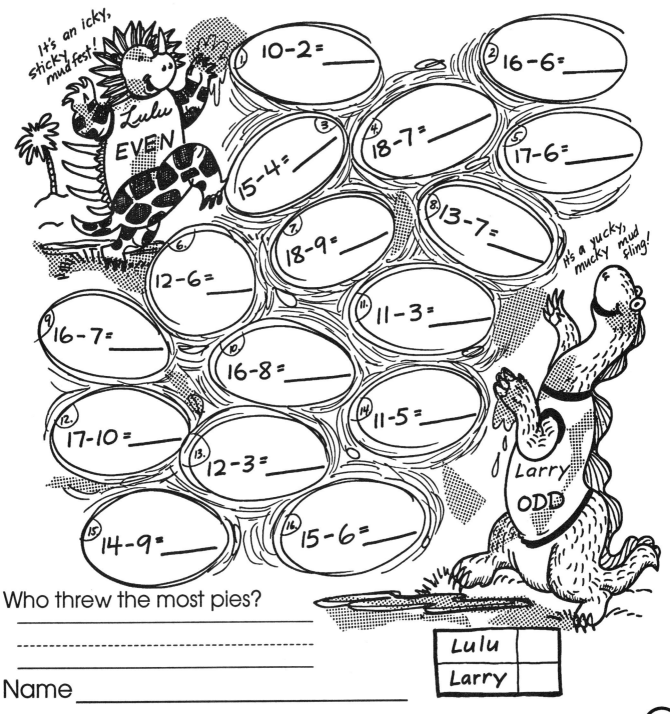

It's an icky, sticky, mud fest!

Lulu
EVEN

It's a yucky, mucky mud fling!

Larry
ODD

1. 10 − 2 = _____
2. 16 − 6 = _____
3. 15 − 4 = _____
4. 18 − 7 = _____
5. 17 − 6 = _____
6. 12 − 6 = _____
7. 18 − 9 = _____
8. 13 − 7 = _____
9. 16 − 7 = _____
10. 16 − 8 = _____
11. 11 − 3 = _____
12. 17 − 10 = _____
13. 12 − 3 = _____
14. 11 − 5 = _____
15. 14 − 9 = _____
16. 15 − 6 = _____

Who threw the most pies?

_____

- -

_____

Name _____

| Lulu | |
| Larry | |

Subtraction Facts through 18

Thirsty Runners

9 runners ran 9 miles.
They dried off with 9 towels.

They drank 9 bottles of juice
and ate 9 candy bars.

All these problems
are about 9.

Find the answers.

1. 12
    − 9
    ___

2. 18
    − 9
    ___

3. 10
    + 9
    ___

4. 13
    − 9
    ___

5. 16
    − 9
    ___

6.   9
    + 4
    ___

7.   9
    + 5
    ___

8. 15
    − 9
    ___

9. 10
    − 9
    ___

10. 17
    − 9
    ___

11. 16
    − 9
    ___

12. 12
    − 3
    ___

13.   9
    − 1
    ___

14. 11
    − 9
    ___

15. 14
    − 9
    ___

16.   9
    + 9
    ___

17.   9
    − 0
    ___

18.   9
    − 9
    ___

Name _____

Addition & Subtraction Facts with 9

Basic Skills/Math K-1

Skateboard Fun

The creatures are having such fun on their skateboards!

Dixon the dinosaur is letting them use his back for their ride.

Use the clues to solve the puzzle.

Write the answer to each number fact in the correct spaces.

CLUES

Across			Down	
A. 10 + 9	D. 10 + 10	G. 7 + 7	A. 9 + 7	F. 6 + 8
B. 8 + 8	E. 7 + 6	H. 5 + 7	C. 4 + 6	G. 5 + 6
C. 9 + 9	F. 8 + 9		E. 8 + 7	H. 2 + 8

Name _____

Addition Facts through 20

Floating Away

Bert was selling balloons at the ballpark.
That was before a big wind came along and blew him away!
Write the answers on his balloons
to help him sink back to Earth.
Then follow the **Color
Code** to color
the balloons.

1.
$$7 + 9$$

2.
$$8 + 9$$

3.
$$16 - 9$$

4.
$$6 + 7$$

5.
$$12 - 5$$

6.
$$14 - 9$$

7.
$$11 - 4$$

8.
$$8 + 8$$

9.
$$12 - 4$$

10.
$$9 + 6$$

11.
$$8 + 6$$

12.
$$8 - 7$$

13.
$$10 - 3$$

14.
$$13 - 8$$

15.
$$11 - 5$$

Color Code	
= 14	Color yellow
< 14	Color blue
> 14	Color red

Name _____

Addition & Subtraction Facts through 20

Help!

6 families are worried! A family member has fallen out of each raft. All the rafts are full of fact families.
Look at the problems on the side of each raft.
Decide what number is missing from both problems.
Draw a line from each raft to its lost family member.

1. $6 + \boxed{} = 10$
   $10 - \boxed{} = 6$

2. $12 - 3 = \boxed{}$
   $\boxed{} + 3 = 12$

3. $2 + \boxed{} = 7$
   $7 - 2 = \boxed{}$

4. $11 - \boxed{} = 5$
   $5 + \boxed{} = 11$

5. $13 - \boxed{} = 6$
   $\boxed{} + 6 = 13$

6. $17 - \boxed{} = 9$
   $9 + \boxed{} = 17$

Name _____

Fact Families

High-Flying Facts

Watch the flying bat family! They are doing tricks for the swamp animals. Each bat has a fact family on its chest. Write the missing numbers in each fact family.

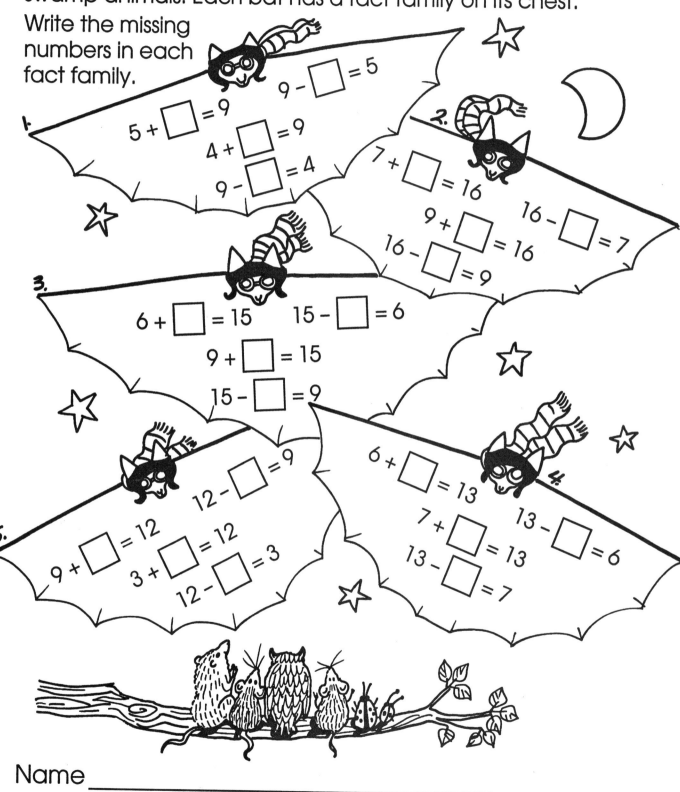

1.
$9 - \boxed{} = 5$
$5 + \boxed{} = 9$
$4 + \boxed{} = 9$
$9 - \boxed{} = 4$

2.
$7 + \boxed{} = 16$
$16 - \boxed{} = 7$
$9 + \boxed{} = 16$
$16 - \boxed{} = 9$

3.
$6 + \boxed{} = 15$
$15 - \boxed{} = 6$
$9 + \boxed{} = 15$
$15 - \boxed{} = 9$

5.
$12 - \boxed{} = 9$
$9 + \boxed{} = 12$
$3 + \boxed{} = 12$
$12 - \boxed{} = 3$

4.
$6 + \boxed{} = 13$
$13 - \boxed{} = 6$
$7 + \boxed{} = 13$
$13 - \boxed{} = 7$

Name _____

Gerbils in the Gym

The gerbils try out everything at the gym.
They balance on the beam and swing from the rings.
They tumble on the mat and swing on the bars.
Count the number of gerbils at each place in the gym.
Write number sentences to solve the gerbil problems.

gerbils on the beam + gerbils on the rings = 9

6 + 3 = 9

rings

beam

mat

bars

1. bars + mat = ☐
    ☐ + ☐ = ☐

2. mat + beam = ☐
    ☐ + ☐ = ☐

3. bars + beam = ☐
    ☐ + ☐ = ☐

4. beam – rings = ☐
    ☐ – ☐ = ☐

5. rings + bars = ☐
    ☐ + ☐ = ☐

6. mat – rings = ☐
    ☐ – ☐ = ☐

Name _____

Number Sentences that Match Models

The Sardine Squeeze

So many sardines have come to watch the underwater ball game!
Will they all fit in the ballpark?
Write a number sentence to match each sardine fact below

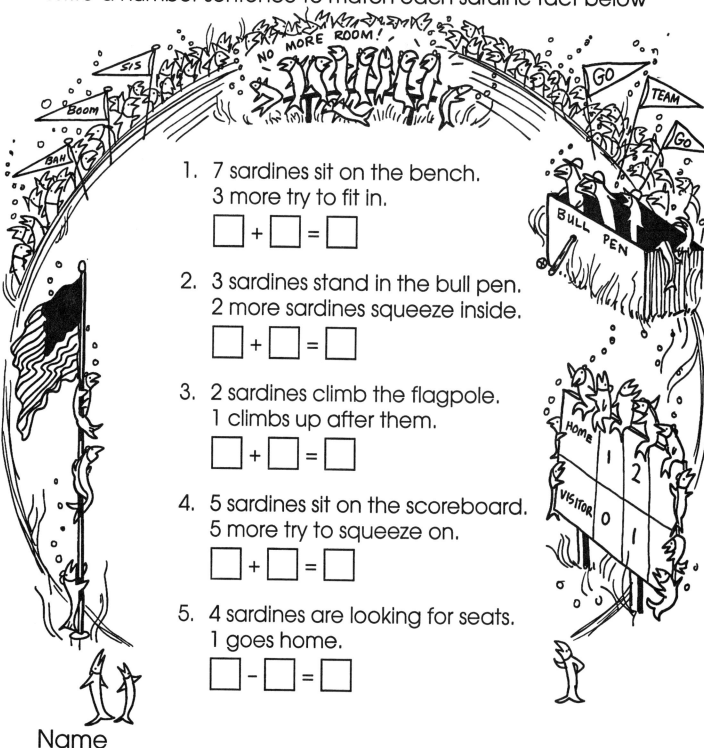

1. 7 sardines sit on the bench.
   3 more try to fit in.

   ☐ + ☐ = ☐

2. 3 sardines stand in the bull pen.
   2 more sardines squeeze inside.

   ☐ + ☐ = ☐

3. 2 sardines climb the flagpole.
   1 climbs up after them.

   ☐ + ☐ = ☐

4. 5 sardines sit on the scoreboard.
   5 more try to squeeze on.

   ☐ + ☐ = ☐

5. 4 sardines are looking for seats.
   1 goes home.

   ☐ – ☐ = ☐

Name _____

Number Sentences that Match Models

Basic Skills/Math K-1

10 Pin Math

When Rosie goes bowling, she wants to knock down all 10 pins.

Look at her scorecard to see how she is doing.

Fill in the missing numbers on her scorecard.

Scorecard

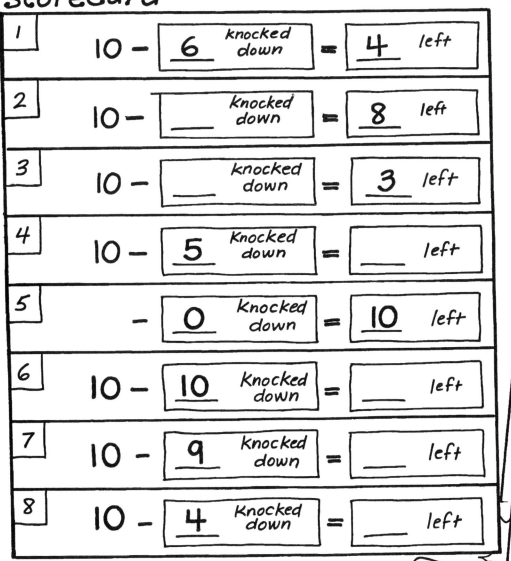

1	10 − 6 knocked down	= 4 left
2	10 − ___ knocked down	= 8 left
3	10 − ___ knocked down	= 3 left
4	10 − 5 knocked down	= ___ left
5	___ − 0 knocked down	= 10 left
6	10 − 10 knocked down	= ___ left
7	10 − 9 knocked down	= ___ left
8	10 − 4 knocked down	= ___ left

Name _____

Find Missing Numbers

Turtle Bridges

The turtles are such good friends to the little mice!
They are building bridges to help the mice cross the river.
Write the missing numbers on the turtle bridges.

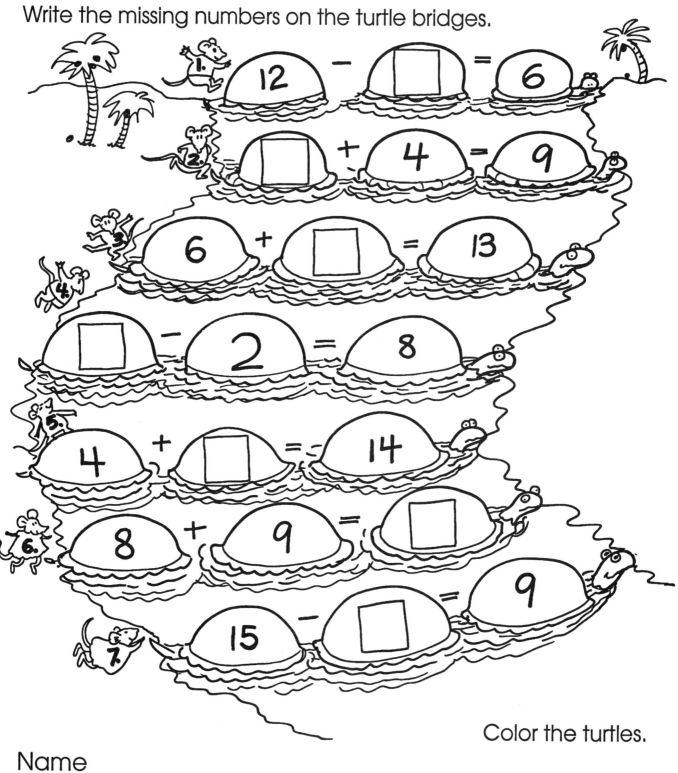

1. $12 - \square = 6$

2. $\square + 4 = 9$

3. $6 + \square = 13$

4. $\square - 2 = 8$

5. $4 + \square = 14$

6. $8 + 9 = \square$

7. $15 - \square = 9$

Color the turtles.

Name _____

Find Missing Numbers

Nothing to Do

Zak found Zeke sitting in a mud hole with nothing to do.
Zero is a number that means nothing.

When you add or subtract 0, the number stays the same.
$6 + 0 = 6$ $\qquad\qquad$ $6 - 0 = 6$

Write the answers to these zero problems.

1. 1   2. 10   3. 100   4. 9   5. 99   6. 999   7. 1000   8. 1000
   +0   +0   +0   −0   −0   −0   +0   −0

9. $0 - 0 = \boxed{}$ 11. Zero − Zero = $\boxed{}$

10. $0 + 0 = \boxed{}$ 12. Zero + Zero = $\boxed{}$

Name _____

The Race of the Swamp Serpents

Which serpent will win the big race?
The winner is the serpent with the largest sum.
Add all 3 numbers on each serpent to find
the sums.

The winner is
_ _ _ _ _ _ _ _

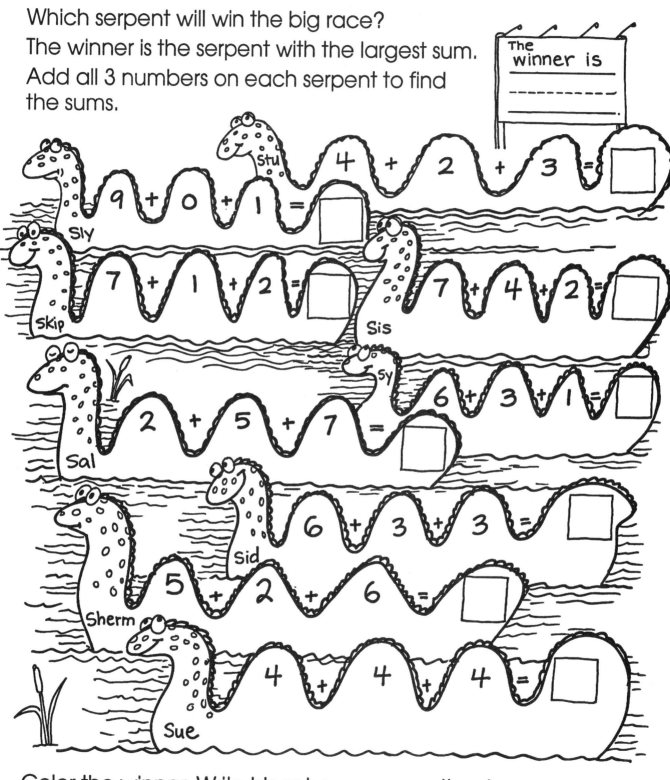

Stu: $4 + 2 + 3 = \boxed{}$

Sly: $9 + 0 + 1 = \boxed{}$

Skip: $7 + 1 + 2 = \boxed{}$

Sis: $7 + 4 + 2 = \boxed{}$

Sy: $6 + 3 + 1 = \boxed{}$

Sal: $2 + 5 + 7 = \boxed{}$

Sid: $6 + 3 + 3 = \boxed{}$

Sherm: $5 + 2 + 6 = \boxed{}$

Sue: $4 + 4 + 4 = \boxed{}$

Color the winner. Write his or her name on the sign.

Name _____

Mystery on Ice

Buzz and Fuzz think they can win the ice-carving contest.
What are they carving?
Find the answers to the problems.
Follow the **Color Code** to color the spaces.
Then you'll see what they are carving!

Color Code
Answers > 10 = yellow
Answers < 10 = blue

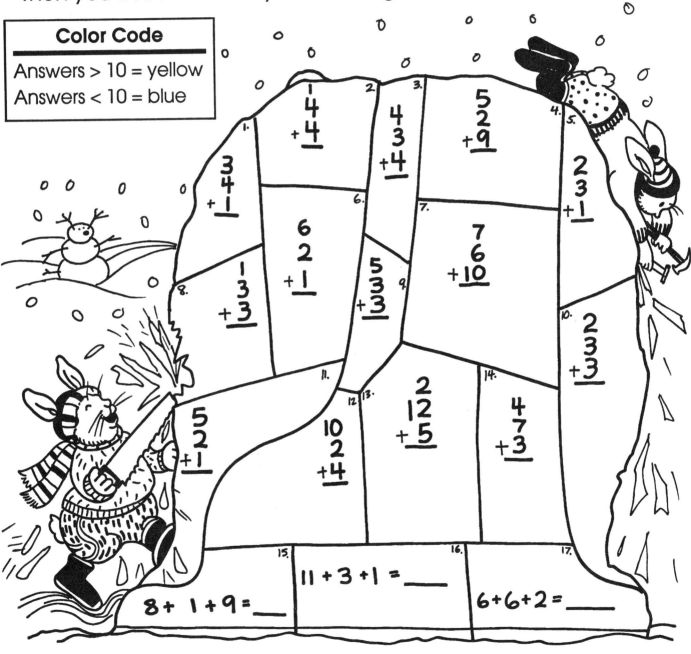

Name _____

Adding 3 Numbers

Checker Problems

Spike is teaching Zip how to play checkers.
He is telling Zip what to do with the checkers.
In math problems, the signs tell you what to do with the numbers.
The signs are missing from all these problems.
You need to put them back!

+ says add.
– says subtract.

Write + or – in each .

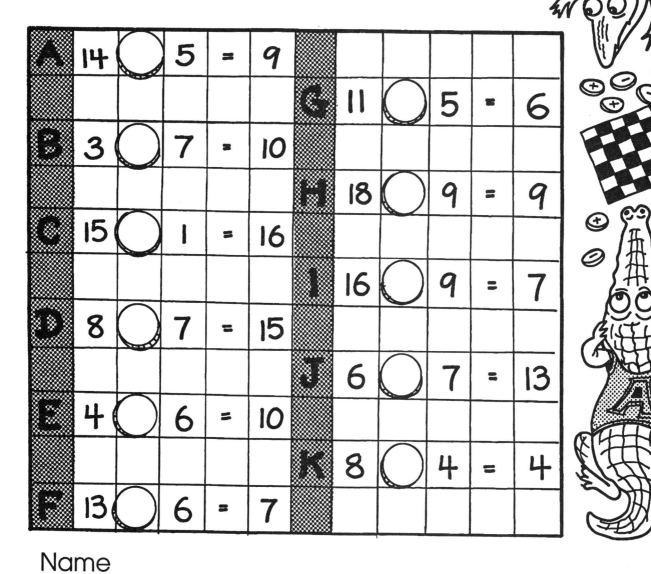

A. $14 \bigcirc 5 = 9$

B. $3 \bigcirc 7 = 10$

C. $15 \bigcirc 1 = 16$

D. $8 \bigcirc 7 = 15$

E. $4 \bigcirc 6 = 10$

F. $13 \bigcirc 6 = 7$

G. $11 \bigcirc 5 = 6$

H. $18 \bigcirc 9 = 9$

I. $16 \bigcirc 9 = 7$

J. $6 \bigcirc 7 = 13$

K. $8 \bigcirc 4 = 4$

Name _____

Choose Correct Operation

Bubbles to Juggle

Did you ever see seals juggle?
These seals juggle sea bubbles for fun!
They also count and add the bubbles as they play.
Solve these bubble problems.

Write each answer in the bubble.

Color the bubbles blue.

Color the rest of the picture, too!

Name _____

Add 2-Digit Numbers

T-Shirts for T-Ball

These little frogs forgot the name of their T-ball team! Help them remember by finding the answers to the T-shirt problems.
Each answer matches a letter in the **Code Box**.
Write the letter on the shirt.
Then read the name of the team.

Code Box

23	= S
38	= G
28	= F
41	= L
66	= E
73	= O
79	= T
85	= R
29	= H

1.
$$68 + 11 = 79$$
T

2.
$$26 + 3$$

3.
$$44 + 22$$

4.
$$15 + 13$$

5.
$$53 + 32$$

6.
$$32 + 41$$

7.
$$16 + 22$$

8.
$$31 + 10$$

9.
$$53 + 13$$

10.
$$14 + 24$$

11.
$$11 + 12$$

What is the name of the team? _____

Name _____

Add 2-Digit Numbers

Look out Below!

Look out for the snowbank!
The bobsled is headed straight for the snowbank.
Solve all the problems to stop the sled before it crashes!

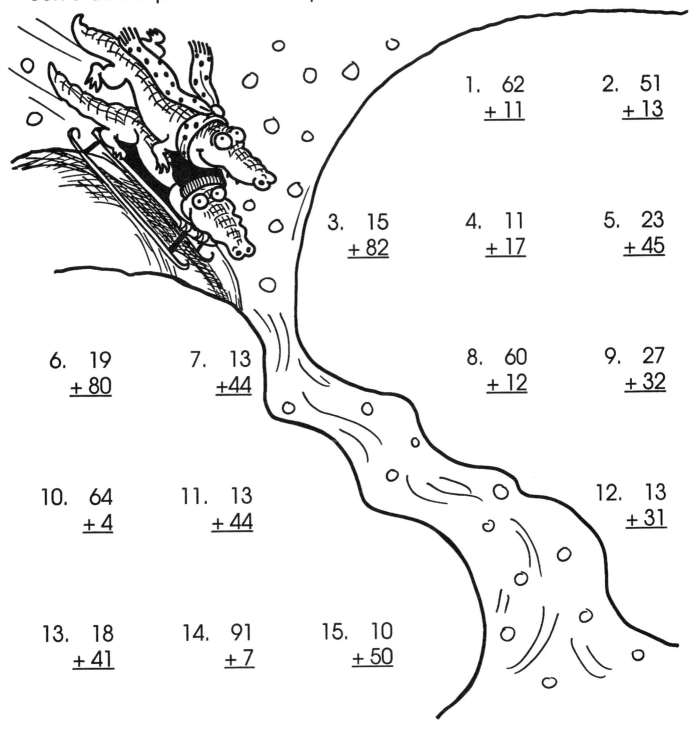

1. 62
   + 11

2. 51
   + 13

3. 15
   + 82

4. 11
   + 17

5. 23
   + 45

6. 19
   + 80

7. 13
   + 44

8. 60
   + 12

9. 27
   + 32

10. 64
    + 4

11. 13
    + 44

12. 13
    + 31

13. 18
    + 41

14. 91
    + 7

15. 10
    + 50

Name _____

Add 2-Digit Numbers

Smashing Fun

Some swamp critters are playing a smashing game of croquet.
Find the answers to the problems on the croquet balls.
Then follow the **Color Code** to color the balls.

Color Code

Fig is 13. Color each 13 ball green.
Mingo is 14. Color each 14 ball orange.
Di is 15. Color each 15 ball blue.
Tut is 16. Color each 16 ball purple.

smash!

Bonk!

Say Cro-kay.

Bang!

whizz

Clunk!

Boink

Color the critter who smashed the most balls.

1. 25 − 12

2. 25 − 10

3. 17 − 1

4. 46 − 30

5. 16 − 2

6. 19 − 3

7. 15 − 2

8. 28 − 14

9. 29 − 14

10. 36 − 20

11. 19 − 6

Name _____

Subtract 2-Digit Numbers

Skating Figure Eights

Cindy Lou and Cy love to skate.

When they skate, they make a lot of eights on the ice.

Solve all the problems.

Check the answers for eights.

How many eights did you find? ☐

1. $12 - 4$

2. $13 - 2$

3. $19 - 11$

4. $46 - 12$

5. $55 - 25$

6. $17 + 40$

7. $21 + 5$

8. $18 - 10$

9. $10 + 50$

10. $68 - 60$

11. $15 + 11$

12. $55 - 22$

13. $18 + 11$

14. $72 + 20$

15. $22 - 11$

16. $28 - 10$

Name _____

Add & Subtract 2-Digit Numbers

Tug-of-War

Tug and pull! Pull and tug!
Who will end up in the mud puddle?
Find the answer to each problem.
Then draw a line to the right answer
on one of the shirts.

1. 12
    + 10

2. 3
    + 10

3. 37
    + 10

4. 16
    + 10

5. 35
    + 10

6. 23
    + 10

7. 7
    + 10

8. 27
    + 10

9. 10
    + 55

10. 58
    + 10

TEAM 1

TEAM 2

Which team do you think will
end up in the mud puddle?

_____
- -
_____

Why do you think so?

_____
- -
_____

Name _____

Add Tens

Basic Skills/Math K-1

Dinosaur Hopscotch

Play hopscotch with the dinosaurs.
Toss a penny 2 times on the board for each problem.
Add the numbers.
Use the spaces below to find the answers.

1. **30** + **40** = **70**
2. ____ + ____ = ____
3. ____ + ____ = ____
4. ____ + ____ = ____
5. ____ + ____ + ____ = ____
6. ____ + ____ = ____

Name _____

Add Multiples of Ten

The Alligator Races

Cheer for your favorite alligator team!

The swamp critters are watching the alligator races.

Find the answers to the problems on the umbrellas.

Then color the umbrellas by following the **Color Code.**

Color Code
10 = yellow
20 = orange
30 = blue
40 = green

Team 1 colors are _____

Team 2 colors are _____

Team 3 colors are _____

Name _____

Subtract Multiples of Ten

Copyright ©1998 by Incentive Publications, Inc., Nashville, TN.
Basic Skills/Math K-1

Happy Hedgehogs

After the badminton game, the hedgehogs went to the Swamp Shack for snacks.

They were happy to find so many tasty treats.

Write a number sentence to show how much money each hedgehog spent.

Gummy Worms 10¢

Candy Crickets 2¢

Taffy Beetles 3¢

Chocolate Ants 5¢

Hank	🐜 + 🐛 =
	☐¢ + ☐¢ = ☐¢

Haley	🦗 + 🪲 =
	☐¢ + ☐¢ = ☐¢

Hattie	🐛 + 🪲 =
	☐¢ + ☐¢ = ☐¢

Hal	🐜 🐜 + 🦗 🦗 =
	☐¢ + ☐¢ = ☐¢

Harry	🐛 🐛 + 🐜 🐜 =
	☐¢ + ☐¢ = ☐¢

Name _____

Problem Solving with Money

A Mouse in a Machine

The little mice love the new pinball machine.
They like it because it looks like a mouse!
Moe the mouse is made of coins.
Every time the mice play the game, the balls hit different coins.
Use the picture on page 41 to solve these money problems.

Write or circle the correct answer.

1. Moe's ears are worth ☐ ¢ together.

2. Moe's eyes are worth ☐ ¢ together.

3. Which is worth more?
   (Circle one.)

   Moe's eyes   **Moe's arms**

4. Each of Moe's legs is worth ☐ ¢.

5. Moe's tummy is worth ☐ ¢.

Circle > for greater than or < for less than.

6. Moe's eyes + ears	>	<	$ 1.00
7. Moe's 2 arms + nose	>	<	$ 1.00
8. Moe's legs + eyes	>	<	$ 1.00
9. Moe's ears + nose	>	<	$ 1.00
10. Moe's tummy + arms	>	<	$ 1.00

Name _____

Problem Solving with Money

Use this picture to help you solve the problems on page 40.

Problem Solving with Money

Join the Rat Race

Help these three fast rats get through the money maze!

For each rat, draw a path from coin to coin.

Use a different color for each path.

Add up the money on each path. Write the total on the finish line.

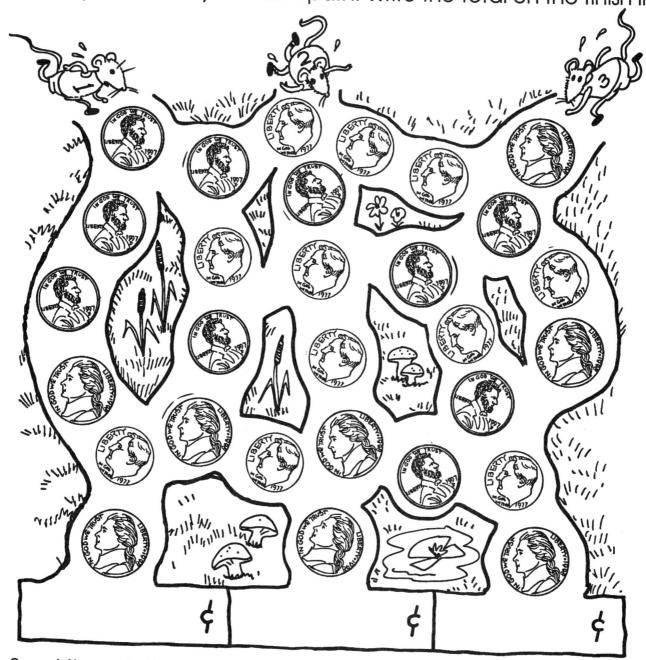

Send the rats through the maze again. Find new paths this time!

Name _____

Problem Solving with Money

Basic Skills/Math K-1

Hold Your Breath!

It's hard to hold your breath for a long time underwater!
These three friends are having a contest to see which one can hold her breath the longest.

Help Freddy Fish mark their times on the timeline.

1. Draw a pink dot on the timeline for flamingo's time.

2. Draw a green dot for turtle's time.

3. Draw a blue dot for whale's time.

4. Color the animal that can hold its breath the longest blue.

5. Color the animal that needs to breathe most often pink.

6. Color the animal that does not need to hold its breath orange.

Name _____

Problem Solving with Time

Cycle Time

Time is so important in a bicycle race!
These riders need your help to keep the time.
Draw the hands on each clock to show the right time.

The race begins at 8 o'clock.

The winner crosses the finish line at 10:30.

Oh, boy! I won!

The last cyclist finishes at 11:00.

1. How long did it take the fastest rider to finish? (Circle one.)
2 hours   2½ hours   3 hours

2. How long did the slowest rider take? (Circle one.)
½ hour   1 hour   3 hours

Name _____

Problem Solving with Time

Copyright ©1998 by INCENTIVE PUBLICATIONS, Inc., Nashville, TN.
Basic Skills/Math K-1

Friends on Wheels

It's a good afternoon for being out on wheels.
Amy and Alex are doing their favorite sports on Crocodile Lane.
Answer the questions about their time on wheels.

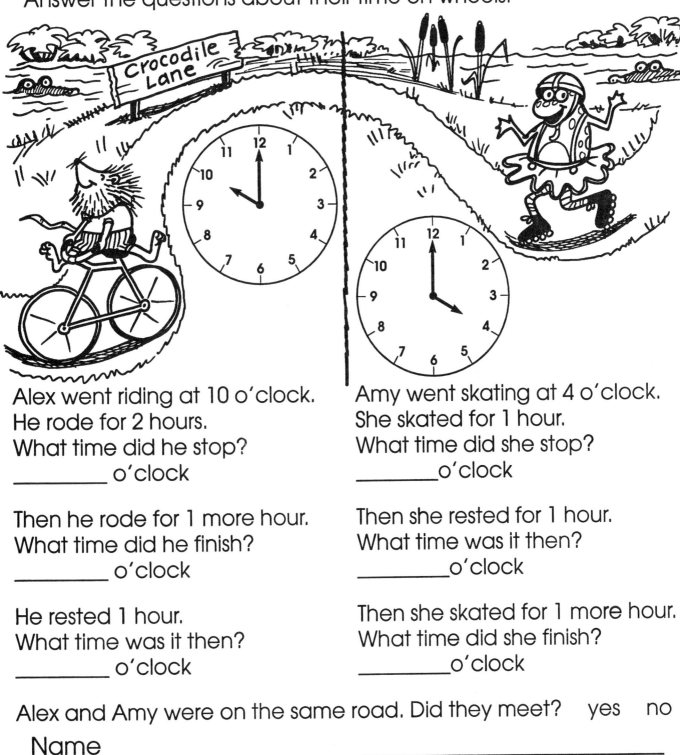

Alex went riding at 10 o'clock.
He rode for 2 hours.
What time did he stop?
_____ o'clock

Then he rode for 1 more hour.
What time did he finish?
_____ o'clock

He rested 1 hour.
What time was it then?
_____ o'clock

Amy went skating at 4 o'clock.
She skated for 1 hour.
What time did she stop?
_____o'clock

Then she rested for 1 hour.
What time was it then?
_____o'clock

Then she skated for 1 more hour.
What time did she finish?
_____o'clock

Alex and Amy were on the same road. Did they meet?   yes   no

Name _____

Problem Solving with Time

A Full Calendar

What day is soccer practice?

Sam has very busy days.

Just look at his calendar on the next page (page 47).

He plays soccer many days in September.

There are lots of other things to do, too!

Fill in the missing dates on the calendar.

Then follow the directions and answer the questions.

1. Count the number of Tuesdays in this month.

2. How many days are between Monday and Friday?

3. Sam has a soccer game every Saturday. Draw ⚽ on those days.

4. Sam visits his grandma on September 25. Draw a ☺ on that day.

5. Sam will wash his dad's car on the first Saturday. What will the date be?

6. Sam goes swimming on September 11. What day is that?

7. School starts on September 8. What day is that?

8. What is the date of his mom's birthday?

Name _____

Use with page 47.

Problem Solving with Time

Write the missing dates on the calendar.

SEPTEMBER

Sunday	Monday	Tuesday	Wednesday	Thursday	Friday	Saturday
		1	2		Swamp Town Picnic	
6 Soccer practice 3:30 at Cattail Field	First day of Critter School		9	10 One last swim in the mud hole ☹		12
Go to the Sea Serpent Races!! 5:00 P.M.	Soccer	15	16 Mom's Birthday (It's a surprise!) Shhhh			19 Clean up the den.
20 Whole family goes to the Daredevil Bat Show. oh, boy!	Soccer	22	23 Bowling with Pee Wee 7:00			
	Soccer	School Field Trip to the Tar Pits. (great)	30 The last day of the month.			

Sam's birthday is on September 6.

Draw a 🎂 on that day.

Name _____

Problem Solving with Time

Weather Watch

The dinosaurs wanted warm, sunny weather for their Dino Olympics.
What kind of weather did they have?

Weather Chart

Kinds of Weather

	NUMBER OF DAYS							
	1	2	3	4	5	6	7	8
1. Rainy	▨	▨	▨	▨				
2. Sunny	▨	▨	▨	▨	▨	▨		
3. Windy	▨	▨	▨	▨	▨	▨		
4. Cloudy	▨	▨	▨	▨	▨			
5. Cold	▨	▨						

They made a graph of the weather
for all the days.
Read the graph to see what the weather was like.
Answer the questions.

1. How many days were rainy? ☐

2. How many days were sunny? ☐

3. How many days were windy? ☐

4. How many days were cloudy? ☐

5. Were there more cold or rainy days? (Circle one.) **cold   rainy**

6. Which kind of weather happened most often? _____

Name _____

Copyright ©1998 by INCENTIVE PUBLICATIONS, Inc., Nashville, TN.
Basic Skills/Math K-1

Horsing Around

It's time for the horseshoe contest! Each game has 2 players.
Peanut has been the champion for 2 years.
Will she win today?
Circle the winner in each game.

score

Game One	
Peanut	21
Smoky	14

Game Two	
Silver	16
Flash	21

Game Three	
Thunder	21
Lightning	11

score

Game Four	
Peanut	21
Thunder	12

Game Five	
Flash	18
Smoky	21

Game Six	
Lightning	21
Silver	19

1. What was the lowest score? ☐

2. How many games did Lightning win? ☐

3. How many games did Silver win? ☐

4. The animal that won the most games is the champion.
   Is Peanut still the champion?   yes   no

Name _____

Problem Solving with a Chart

Keeping Score

The Stompers were sure their team would win the big game.
The Mashers were sure their team would win the big game.
Now the game is over.
Read the scoreboard to see how each team did in the game.

Quarters	Stompers	Mashers
1st quarter	7	7
2nd quarter	10	7
3rd quarter	16	10
4th quarter	16	17

Circle the correct answer.

1. The Stompers were ahead in the **(1st & 2nd, 2nd & 3rd)** quarters.

2. The teams were tied in the **(1st, 2nd, 3rd)** quarter.

3. The Mashers were ahead in the **(1st, 3rd, 4th)** quarter.

4. The Stompers' score was the same in the **(1st & 3rd, 3rd & 4th)** quarter.

5. The winning team was _____

Name _____

Basic Skills/Math K-1

The Fly Ball

Over the fence comes the ball!
Someone hit a home run at the ball field.
The ball went flying over the fence into the park.
Use the picture to help find the ball.
Answer the questions about the park.

Circle the correct answer.

1. The ball's first bounce is near the   **swings   picnic table   sandbox**

2. Which is closest to the fence?
   park benches   restrooms   drinking fountain

3. The ball's second bounce is near the
   fence   merry-go-round   teeter-totter

4. The swings are closest to the   **sandbox   benches   restrooms**

5. The ball has stopped near the   **swings   tree   restrooms**

Name _____

Problem Solving with an Illustration

The Sports Lover

Bookworm is just crazy about sports books.

He can't stop reading!

Answer each question about his book reading habit.

Write a problem to help you find each answer.

1. He read 2 books on Monday and 4 books on Tuesday. How many books did he read on those 2 days?

   ☐ + ☐ = ☐

2. On Wednesday he read 5 books. On Thursday he read 6 more. How many books did he read on those 2 days?

   ☐ + ☐ = ☐

3. On Friday he piled up the books he read all week. How many were in the pile?

   ☐ + ☐ = ☐

4. On Saturday, he counted all the books he owned. He had 27. He gave away 5 books. How many did he have left?

   ☐ – ☐ = ☐

Bookworm read his pile of books twice.

Then he ate them!

Name _____

Reading about sports is my <u>favorite</u> sport.

Spring Cleaning

Pack Rat, why are you throwing away all this great stuff?
Look at everything Pack Rat found when he cleaned his room.
Read the sentences below.
Write a number sentence for each one,
and find the answer.

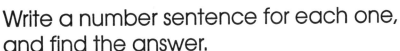

1. He found a baseball bat and a glove.

   ☐ 1 ☐ + ☐ 1 ☐ = ☐ 2 ☐

2. He found a snorkel and 2 swim fins.

   ☐ + ☐ = ☐

3. He found a basketball and 2 soccer balls.

   ☐ + ☐ = ☐

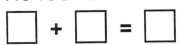

4. He found 2 rollerblades,
   a skateboard, and a helmet.

   ☐ + ☐ + ☐ = ☐

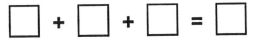

5. He found a crazy hat and a baseball.

   ☐ + ☐ = ☐

Name _____

Word Problems

A Wild River Ride

Hang on tight!

The water is moving fast!

Someone has fallen off the raft!

Write number sentences to solve all the problems about the wild river ride.

1. The raft had 5 riders. 1 fell off. How many are left?

2. The friends built the raft in 4 days. They painted it for 2 days. How long did it take to get the raft ready?

3. The animals rode the raft for 2 hours. Then they had a picnic for 1 hour. How long were they together?

4. The friends took 2 raft trips on Monday. They took 1 raft trip on Tuesday. They took 3 raft trips on Wednesday. How many raft trips did they take?

Name _____

Word Problems

Basic Skills/Math K-1

Spinning Problems

The merry-go-round makes these friends dizzy.

Play a spinning game that won't get you dizzy!

Make a spinner with a paper clip and your pencil.

See the picture at the top of the page.

Spin the paper clip with your finger.

Watch where it stops.

Spin the paper clip 3 times to get 3 numbers.

Make a problem with the numbers.

Use + or – or both!

Sample: 8 + 4 – 2 = 10

Keep spinning to make 4 problems.

1. _____   3. _____

2. _____   4. _____

Name _____

Two-Point Hoops

Fritz and Fran are shooting hoops.
You and a friend can play, too.
Put this paper on a desk in front of you.
Take turns tossing the penny into the net.
Each of you should toss the penny 5 times.
Score 2 points for each basket.
Score 0 points for each miss.

Your Score

1 _____

2 _____

3 _____

4 _____

5 _____

Total _____

Friend's Score

1 _____

2 _____

3 _____

4 _____

5 _____

Total _____

What would your score be if you never missed? _____

Explain how you solved this problem.

Name _____

Explain Solutions to Problems

High-Jumping Jumpers

All of these animals are prize-winning jumpers.

Who jumped the highest today?

Read all the clues.

Then tell who jumped the highest.

whopeeee

HIGH
JUMP

CLUES

Cricket jumps higher than rabbit.

Rabbit does not jump as high as frog.

Frog does not jump as high as cricket.

Who jumps the highest? _____

Explain how you got your answer. _____

_____

_____

_____

_____

_____

_____

_____

Name _____

Using Logic to Solve Problems

Math Computation & Problem Solving Skills Test

Write the answers.

1. + = ☐

2. − = ☐

3. $3 + 3 =$ ☐   4. $7 - 2 =$ ☐   5. $6 + 4 =$ ☐

6. $9 - 6 =$ ☐   7. $5 + 5 =$ ☐

8. − = ☐ ¢

9. = ☐ ¢

10. 7	11. 9	12. 8	13. 12	14. 5
+ 4	− 5	+ 8	− 4	+ 8

15. 10	16. 4	17. 10	18. 6	19. 13
− 7	+ 9	− 7	+ 2	− 4

Name _____

Math Computation & Problem Solving Skills Test Copyright ©1998 by Incentive Publications, Inc., Nashville, TN.
Basic Skills/Math K-1

Write a number sentence to go with each picture.

20.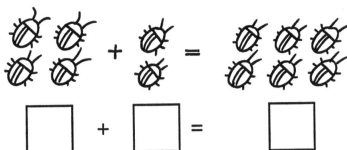

[ ] + [ ] = [ ]

21.

[ ] + [ ] − [ ] = [ ]

Write the missing numbers.

22. $\boxed{} - 7 = 9$

23. $8 + \boxed{} = 10$

24. $\boxed{} - 3 = 6$

25. $6 + \boxed{} = 12$

26. $\boxed{} + 3 = 8$

27. $\boxed{} + 5 = 11$

28. $6 + \boxed{} = 15$

29. $\boxed{} + 9 = 11$

30. $17 - \boxed{} = 10$

31. $\boxed{} + 8 = 15$

32. What time does the clock show? _____ o'clock

33. What time will it be in 2 hours? _____ o'clock

Name _____

34. 26	35. 49	36. 12	37. 30	38. 66
+ 3	− 23	+ 6	− 20	+ 10

Write the missing signs + or –.

39. 8 ☐ 6 = 14   40. 4 ☐ 3 = 7   41. 12 ☐ 9 = 3

Look at the chart to answer the questions.

42. What was Sid's time? ☐

43. Who was faster than Sly? (Circle one.)
    Sal   Sue   Sid

44. Who was the slowest? (Circle one.)
    Sal   Sid   Sly   Sue

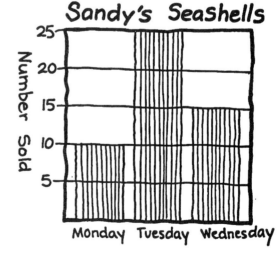

SEA SERPENT RACES	
SWIMMER	TIME
1. Sly	4 min.
2. Sid	6 min.
3. Sal	7 min.
4. Sue	3 min.

Look at the graph to answer the questions.

45. Which day did Sandy sell the
    most shells? (Circle one.)
    Monday   Tuesday   Wednesday

46. How many shells did
    Sandy sell on Monday? ☐

Name _____

Math Computation & Problem Solving Skills Test Copyright ©1998 by Incentive Publications, Inc., Nashville, TN.
Basic Skills/Math K-1

Write a problem to find the answers.

47. Dino scored 27 points in the first game.

    He scored 10 points in the second game.

    How many points did he score in all?

48. Mimi fell 12 times on Monday.

    She fell 5 times on Tuesday.

    She fell 2 times on Wednesday.

    How many times did she fall all together?

49. Frog brought 14 candy bars to diving class.

    He gave 7 away.

    How many did he have left?

50. Tom had $35 in his turtle bank.

    He spent $22 on new skates.

    How much money does he have left?

Name _____

Answer Key

Skills Test

1. 7	29. 2
2. 5	30. 7
3. 6	31. 7
4. 5	32. 10
5. 10	33. 6
6. 3	34. 29
7. 10	35. 26
8. 20¢	36. 18
9. 56¢	37. 10
10. 11	38. 76
11. 4	39. +
12. 16	40. +
13. 8	41. –
14. 13	42. 6
15. 3	43. Sue
16. 13	44. Sal
17. 3	45. Tuesday
18. 8	46. 10
19. 9	47. 27
20. 4 + 2 = 6	+10
21. 3 + 3 – 1 = 5	37
22. 16	48. 12
23. 2	5
24. 9	+2
25. 6	19
26. 5	49. 14 – 7 = 7
27. 6	50. $ 35
28. 9	– $ 22
	$ 13

Skills Exercises

page 10

1. 7
2. 10
3. 12
4. 13

page 11

1. 2	5. 1
2. 4	6. 4
3. 4	7. 1
4. 1	8. 0

page 12

1. 10
2. 1
3. 9
4. 9 + 10 + 1 = 20

page 13

1. 4
2. 5
3. 3
4. 2
5. 8
6. 4
7. 3
8. 6

The winning score is 8.

page 14

1. 12	10. 12
2. 11	11. 11
3. 12	12. 12
4. 9	13. 8
5. 9	14. 8
6. 8	15. 11
7. 9	# 8 is the
8. 10	lost red
9. 11	boot.

page 15

Missing Numbers
on Chart

Elvis	1
Dino	7
Dinah	3
Danny	12
Sally	12
Emma	5
Rico	10

1. 12	4. 12
2. 5	5. 10
3. 7	6. Elvis

page 16

1. 18	9. 17
2. 18	10. 14
3. 17	11. 16
4. 14	12. 15
5. 16	13. 17
6. 18	14. 17
7. 15	15. 16
8. 14	

page 17

1. 8	9. 9
2. 10	10. 8
3. 11	11. 8
4. 11	12. 7
5. 11	13. 9
6. 6	14. 6
7. 9	15. 5
8. 6	16. 9

Lulu threw 7 mud pies,
and Larry threw 9
mud pies.

Larry threw the most.

Copyright ©1998 by Incentive Publications, Inc., Nashville, TN.
Basic Skills/Math K-1

page 18

1. 3	10. 8
2. 9	11. 7
3. 19	12. 9
4. 4	13. 8
5. 7	14. 2
6. 13	15. 5
7. 14	16. 18
8. 6	17. 9
9. 1	18. 0

page 19

Across	Down
A. 19	A. 16
B. 16	C. 10
C. 18	E. 15
D. 20	F. 14
E. 13	G. 11
F. 17	H. 10
G. 14	
H. 12	

page 20

1. 16	9. 8
2. 17	10. 15
3. 7	11. 14
4. 13	12. 1
5. 7	13. 7
6. 5	14. 5
7. 7	15. 6
8. 16	

page 21

Missing numbers
are:

1. 4	4. 6
2. 9	5. 7
3. 5	6. 8

page 22

1. 4, 4, 5, 5
2. 9, 9, 7, 7
3. 9, 9, 6, 6
4. 7, 7, 6, 6
5. 3, 3, 9, 9

page 23

1. 4 + 5 = 9
2. 5 + 6 = 11
3. 4 + 6 = 10
4. 6 - 3 = 3
5. 3 + 4 = 7
6. 5 – 3 = 2

page 24

1. 7 + 3 = 10
2. 3 + 2 = 5
3. 2 + 1 = 3
4. 5 + 5 = 10
5. 4 –1 = 3

page 25

1. 4	5. 10
2. 2	6. 0
3. 7	7. 1
4. 5	8. 6

page 26

1. 6	5. 10
2. 5	6. 17
3. 7	7. 6
4. 10	

page 27

1. 1	7. 1000
2. 10	8. 1000
3. 100	9. 0
4. 9	10. 0
5. 99	11. 0
6. 999	12. 0

page 28

Stu	9
Sly	10
Skip	10
Sis	13
Sy	10
Sal	14
Sid	12
Sherm	13
Sue	12

The winner is Sal.

page 29

The ice sculpture
will be a skate.
See that all
spaces within
skate are
colored yellow.

page 30

A. –	G. –
B. +	H. –
C. +	I. –
D. +	J. +
E. +	K. –
F. –	

page 31

1. 19	5. 39
2. 27	6. 49
3. 88	7. 96
4. 96	8. 66

page 32

1. 79	7. 38
2. 29	8. 41
3. 66	9. 66
4. 28	10. 38
5. 85	11. 23
6. 73	

The name of the
team is The
Frog Legs.

page 33

1. 73	9. 59
2. 64	10. 68
3. 97	11. 57
4. 28	12. 44
5. 68	13. 59
6. 99	14. 98
7. 57	15. 60
8. 72	

page 34

1. 13	7. 13
2. 15	8. 14
3. 16	9. 15
4. 16	10. 16
5. 14	11. 13
6. 16	

Tut smashed the
most balls.
Check to see
that student
has colored Tut.

page 35

1. 8	9. 60
2. 11	10. 8
3. 8	11. 26
4. 34	12. 33
5. 30	13. 29
6. 57	14. 92
7. 26	15. 11
8. 8	16. 18

There are 4 eights.

page 36

1. 22	6. 33
2. 13	7. 17
3. 47	8. 37
4. 26	9. 65
5. 45	10. 68

Bottom answers
will vary.

page 37

Answers will vary.

page 38

1. 10	7. 30
2. 40	8. 20
3. 40	9. 10
4. 10	10. 20
5. 20	11. 30
6. 30	12. 40

Team colors are:
Team 1—yellow &
green

Team 2—orange & blue
Team 3—yellow, green,
    orange, & blue

page 39

Hank   15¢
Haley   5¢
Hattie 13¢
Hal   14¢
Harry   30¢

pages 40–41

1. 50¢   6. <
2. 20¢   7. <
3. Moe's eyes   8. >
4. 55¢   9. <
5. 35¢   10. <

page 42

Answers will vary.
Check to see that
    student has added
    coins accurately.

page 43

1–3. Check to see that
    student has drawn
    dots in correct spots.
4. Whale—blue
5. Flamingo—pink
6. Fish—orange

page 44

Check to see that
    student has drawn
    hands on the clocks
    accurately.
1. 2 ½ hours
2. 3 hours

page 45

Alex: 12 o'clock,
         1 o'clock,
         2 o'clock
Amy: 5 o'clock,
         6 o'clock,
         7 o'clock
No.

pages 46–47

1. 5
2. 3
3–4. Check to see that
    student followed
    directions correctly.
5. September 5
6. Friday
7. Tuesday
8. September 17

page 48

1. 4
2. 8
3. 6
4. 5
5. rainy
6. sunny

page 49

Circle winners:
Game 1 ....Peanut
Game 2 ....Flash
Game 3 ....Thunder
Game 4 ....Peanut
Game 5 ....Smoky
Game 6 ....Lightning
1. 11
2. 1
3. 0
4. yes

page 50

1. 2nd & 3rd
2. 1st
3. 4th
4. 3rd & 4th
5. Mashers

page 51

1. picnic table
2. drinking fountain
3. teeter-totter
4. sandbox
5. restrooms

page 52

1. $2 + 4 = 6$
2. $5 + 6 = 11$
3. $2 + 4 + 5 + 6 = 17$ or $6 + 11 = 17$
4. $27 - 5 = 22$

page 53

1. $1 + 1 = 2$
2. $1 + 2 = 3$
3. $1 + 2 = 3$
4. $2 + 1 + 1 = 4$
5. $1 + 1 = 2$

page 54

1. $5 - 1 = 4$ riders
2. $4 + 2 = 6$ days
3. $2 + 1 = 3$ hours
4. $2 + 1 + 3 = 6$ trips

page 55

Problems will vary.

page 56

Scores will vary.
Score would be 10.
Explanations will vary.

page 57

Cricket jumps the
    highest.
Explanations will vary.